D0169501

All About
The Grand Canyon

Don Lago

BLUE RIVER PRESS

Indianapolis, Indiana

All About the Grand Canyon
Copyright © 2018 by Don Lago

Published by Blue River Press
Indianapolis, Indiana
www.brpressbooks.com

Distributed by Cardinal Publishers Group
A Tom Doherty Company, Inc.
www.cardinalpub.com

All rights reserved under International and
Pan-American Copyright Conventions.

No part of this book may be reproduced, stored in a database
or other retrieval system, or transmitted in any form, by
any means, including mechanical, photocopy, recording
or otherwise, without the prior written permission of the
publisher.

ISBN: 978-1-68157-100-3
Library of Congress Control Number: 2018943495

Cover Design: David Miles
Book Design: Dave Reed
Cover Artist: Robert Perrish
Editor: Dani McCormick
Illustrator: Alexandra Myers

Printed in the United States of America

7 6 5 4 3 2 1   18 19 20 21 22 23 24

Contents

All About
The Grand Canyon

Preface

It's not just an okay canyon, or a pretty good canyon, or one of many grand canyons, it is THE Grand Canyon. It's the most famous canyon on Earth. The Grand Canyon is a mile deep, ten miles wide, and 277 miles long. At its bottom is a mighty river, the Colorado River.

A city or Yosemite Valley could easily hide inside the Grand Canyon. Four Empire State Buildings would have to stack up to reach the top of the canyon, and twelve Golden Gate Bridges would have to link up to cross it.

The Grand Canyon is full of amazing shapes, colors, and beauty. Looking from the rim and into the canyon, it looks like the canyon is too far away, something that can only be experienced by eyes. But there are lots of ways that people, including kids, can "get personal" with the canyon.

There are hiking trails into the canyon. Mule rides go to the canyon bottom, where people stay overnight in a stone cabin or a tent. Rafting down the Colorado River offers big rapids. Miles of trails along the canyon rim let people walk or ride a bike as much as they want. For amazing views, visitors can take a helicopter ride over the canyon.

The canyon walls are full of fossils of ancient creatures, and the canyon floor and rims are crawling with today's animals. Also in the park are the ruins of ancient Native American houses. A camera or a paintbrush may try, but they can never capture the canyon's magical sunsets. Junior Rangers can go for a walk with a park ranger and get a badge.

The Grand Canyon is full of surprises. Since the Grand Canyon is located in Arizona, people might expect it to be a desert with heat, cacti, and rattlesnakes. But the rim is 7,000 feet above sea level and surrounded by big forests and forest-type wildlife like elk, deer, and mountain lions.

The rim gets lots of snow in the winter. But the canyon bottom, a mile below, is twenty or twenty-five degrees warmer than the rim.

In summer, the canyon bottom is usually 100 degrees, sometimes 115 degrees Fahrenheit. The canyon bottom is indeed a desert with cacti and rattlesnakes.

The canyon is full of amazing human stories. A thousand years ago, Native Americans lived and farmed inside the canyon. In 1869, a guy with only one arm, John Wesley Powell, bravely led the first boat trip through what he called "the Great Unknown."

In the 1880s, prospectors searched the canyon for riches and built trails to their mines. Then Americans realized that the canyon's greatest value was as a natural wonder. They made it into a national park, protecting it for future generations.

The Grand Canyon is all ready for visitors.

Chapter 1

The Grand Canyon is a
Time Machine

National parks are the best places to have adventures, go for hikes, climb a mountain, raft a river, or see wild animals. Visitors aren't watching someone else having adventures in movies or TV. They aren't just pretending that they are having adventures with video games. These places are very real, and now anyone can do something really daring, difficult, and exciting.

Hiking into the Grand Canyon is like having a time machine and traveling into the past. The Grand Canyon is the best place anywhere to see Earth's history. The rocks at the bottom are 1.8 billion years old, or about 40 percent as old as Earth. On top of that are stacked younger layers of rock, like the layers of a birthday cake.

A number like "1.8 billion" is hard to grasp, even for adults. Try this: imagine that a whole year is reduced to the timespan of only one second. By this measure, 3,600 years would fit into one

The Grand Canyon National Park is
in the southwestern part of the United States.

hour, and 270 million years would equal eight
and a half years. The top rock layer of the Grand
Canyon is 270 million years old. Someone who
is sixty years old would contain 1.8 billion years.

Looking into the canyon, you see bands of
different colors. Some are thicker, some thinner.
Some form cliffs, and others form slopes. That
is because there are different types of rocks.
Sandstone is made of sand. Shale forms from
the compaction of silt and clay that we normally
call mud. Limestone is made of the shells and
calcium of ancient sea creatures.

These rocks were created in different
environments—oceans, beaches, swamps, or

deserts—as the world slowly changed. Some rocks are harder and some are softer, so they break down in different ways. The harder rocks form cliffs, and the softer rocks form slopes. When you hike into the canyon, these bands of color become rocks loaded with details.

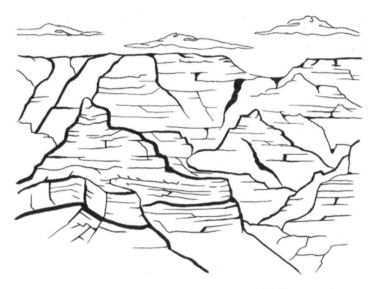

The Grand Canyon has many rock layers of different colors, formed by different types of rocks over a very long time.

The Grand Canyon has a dozen trails that go from the rim to the Colorado River. These trails started as animal trails, then became Native American trails. American prospectors improved the trails for burros and mules. The most popular trail is the Bright Angel Trail, which starts in the middle of Grand Canyon Village.

The cluster of hotels and restaurants that make up Grand Canyon Village is on the canyon's South Rim. Most visitors go to the South Rim, which is closer to highways and stays open all year. The North Rim is 1,000 feet higher than the South Rim and gets so much snow that it closes for more than half the year.

The Bright Angel Trail is the most popular trail at the canyon, attracting many hikers.

The Bright Angel Trail takes about eight miles to descend to the Colorado River. In those eight miles of walking, visitors are dropping one vertical mile—that's steep! Lots of people take short hikes down the trail just to get a feel for what it's like to be inside the canyon. They like looking at the rocks and looking up at the rim.

Visitors can also hike all the way to the bottom, but only if they've made plans to stay there overnight. Hiking in the canyon is hard work, especially coming back up. Plenty of kids have hiked it, and so have people in their nineties, and disabled people with prosthetic legs. A blind park ranger named Keith Green worked at the bottom of the canyon for years and hiked it all the time.

Hikers need some sturdy and worn-in hiking boots, and maybe a hiking pole for better balance. Hikers need to take plenty of water. The biggest danger, especially in summer, is dehydration. Sweating out more water than you are drinking can make you really sick. Many canyon visitors come from other climates and don't understand that a desert climate can dry you out really fast. Dehydration can even kill you.

It's best to hike in the spring or autumn, not summer. One way hikers protect themselves from the sun is by wearing good hats.

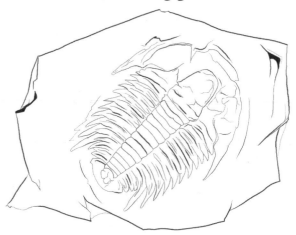

Trilobite fossils have been used to determine the age and movement of rocks.

As soon as Bright Angel Trail starts, many people notice odd shapes in the cliffs. These are fossils of seashells, corals, and sponges. The trail goes right through an ancient ocean! The dead bodies of countless sea creatures piled up on the ocean floor and eventually turned into this limestone.

These fossils are older than the dinosaurs. The canyon doesn't contain any dinosaur bones or fossils because the dinosaurs are youngsters compared to Grand Canyon rocks.

But you don't need to go down the trail to see fossils. One of the park's most popular ranger programs is the "Fossil Walk," which takes visitors to a place on the rim that is packed with fossils. It's like a treasure hunt. The ranger lets people find the fossils, and then talks about the creatures that made them.

Not far down from the rim, the trail goes through a tunnel that was carved through a cliff. Just past the tunnel, under an overhanging ledge, are some pictographs.

After less than a mile, the trail comes to a rock layer that looks different. The canyon's

Pictographs help archaeologists discover how prehistoric people lived and worked.

main color is red, but this layer is white. It has many sloping, crisscrossing lines in it. These are ancient sand dunes.

Most of the canyon's rock layers were created underwater, but this layer was part of a desert. The dune slopes tell geologists which way the wind was blowing 280 million years ago. In places, these rocks hold the fossilized tracks of ancient lizards.

Alert visitors may see not just fossil tracks of lizards or pictographs of desert bighorn sheep. They'll see real, living lizards and desert bighorn sheep scrambling over the rocks.

A little farther and hikers notice their boots turning kind of red as they walk through the dust of rocks formed from mud and sand. This rock has a lot of iron in it, which makes it red. The boots of unlucky hikers may turn a bit green from stepping in poop from the mules that carry riders on the trail.

The tallest cliffs in the canyon are formed by the Redwall Limestone, so it's not surprising that it holds some of the steepest parts of the trail. There aren't many places in the canyon where trails and people can get through the Redwall Limestone cliffs.

Bright Angel Trail follows a geological fault—a crack in the earth's surface. The fault has broken the cliffs and left a massive pile of boulders and dirt. The trail zig zags back and forth over this debris. This allows people to climb down into the canyon.

The Redwall Limestone, like most of the canyon's rocks, was formed in the ocean and then lifted a mile and a half above sea level. How did this happen? Some Native Americans believe that the earth is the shell of a giant turtle, and that earthquakes happen when the turtle moves. In a poetic way, they were right.

Scientists have found that the earth is made of many giant rock shells, called tectonic plates. The powerful heat inside the planet pushes these plates around very slowly. When they collide, they force the land to rise, creating earthquakes, volcanoes, and mountains. Tectonic forces pushed the Grand Canyon's rock layers out of the ocean and high above it.

On the trail, the rocks and dust change color again to gray-green. This is the Bright Angel Shale, 500 million years old. If you know how to recognize them, you can see the fossilized tracks of trilobites, which were like today's horseshoe crabs. Just like people today, the trilobites went for a walk one morning. Their tracks from 500 million years ago tell all about it.

Soon the trail comes to Indian Garden, where hikers can rest beneath cottonwood trees. The trees get their name because their seeds float on little parachutes that look like cotton puffs. From the rim, the cottonwood trees look like little bushes, but up close they are about 100 feet tall.

Trilobites were the first species on Earth to have good eyes, making them so successful that they spread all over the world.

These cottonwoods grow here because springs give them lots of water. As you descend into the canyon, the temperatures get warmer and the plants get smaller and more spread out.

Heading downward again, the trail follows a pretty creek through a narrow sandstone canyon. Then the trail drops steeply again, zig zagging through black cliffs streaked with pink granite. This is some of the oldest rock on Earth, 1.8 billion years old.

To camp at Indian Garden campgrounds, or anywhere below the canyon's rim, visitors have to have a backcountry permit.

Chapter 2
Phantom Ranch

From Phantom Ranch, mules will carry postcards
out of the canyon.

What is that roaring sound ahead? Suddenly
the Colorado River comes into view, with rapids.
This is the force that carved through all this rock
and created the Grand Canyon. The trail follows
the river for another mile, on a ledge in the cliffs,
then crosses a narrow bridge. Hikers can pause
in the middle and look down at the fast-moving
river. Maybe some rafts zip along below.

At last, hikers are done with their journey. The hike ends at Phantom Ranch, where hikers stay at a campground or in cabins. Visitors can eat dinner and breakfast in a stone café and talk with other hikers or people who rode down on mules.

The Ranch sells postcards that say "Mailed by Mule at the Bottom of the Grand Canyon." The people who work at Phantom Ranch work for ten days and then get four days off. They don't get mule rides or helicopter rides in and out of the canyon—they have to hike.

But you don't need to hike into the canyon to get a close look at its rocks. On the rim is the Trail of Time, a 1.4 mile paved trail displaying dozens of boulders brought up from inside the canyon. Many boulders have amazing colors and patterns, and visitors are welcome to touch them. Also on the rim is the Bright Angel Lodge, which includes a fireplace built out of all the rock layers inside the canyon. This fireplace is located in the History Room, a little museum that tells visitors about the imaginative architect, Mary Colter. She designed the fireplace, Bright Angel Lodge, Phantom Ranch, and many other buildings at Grand Canyon National Park.

Visitors at Phantom Ranch eat meals in this stone café.

The name "Bright Angel" is repeated often at the Grand Canyon. This name was given to the creek at the canyon's bottom by John Wesley Powell, who explored the Grand Canyon by boat in 1869. The pretty creek flows past what is now Phantom Ranch. The name later got attached to the trail and the lodge. Powell took the name from a famous hymn that begins "Shall we gather at the river, where bright angel feet have trod."

Many of the peaks inside the canyon have names from the world's religions, such as Buddha Temple, The Tower of Ra, and Apollo Temple. Many of these names were given by Clarence Dutton, a geologist who studied the canyon in the 1870s. Dutton planned to be a minister, but the Civil War gave him a career in the US army,

Clarence Dutton graduated from Yale College before working for the US Geological Survey.

and he helped survey the West. When Dutton saw the Grand Canyon, he saw the greatest forces of creation. He wanted names that would inspire other visitors to see the mystery and glory of creation.

Hiking in the Grand Canyon can leave you feeling pretty small sometimes. But you can also see all the time, all the geological forces, and all the past life from which human lives arose. Every human body contains all of creation.

Chapter 3
The Colorado River

When you stand on the rim of the Grand Canyon and look into its rocky depths, you may not see any motion at all. You could imagine that the canyon is a very dead thing. But the canyon has a wildly beating heart—the Colorado River. The Colorado is a powerful river.

In the course of its journey through the canyon, it falls about 2,000 feet. Niagara Falls drops only 182 feet. The Colorado River falls eleven times as far as Niagara Falls. This fall is spread out over 277 miles, but it includes more than 150 rapids.

The Grand Canyon holds some of the most famous rapids in the world. For river runners (people who love to raft, canoe, or kayak down rivers), the Grand Canyon is the adventure of a lifetime. It's like climbing Mt. Everest or playing in the World Series.

The Colorado River provides water for nearly 40 million people.

Even kids can raft the Colorado River. They can go with a rafting company, which supplies all the equipment, and expert guides who know the river well. Rafts are made out of heavy rubber like tires, so if they scrape against rocks, they should be okay.

Children have to be twelve years old to go on an oar raft, which has a guide who rows long oars. They have to be eight years old to go on a motorized raft, which is bigger than an oar raft and carries more people. An oar raft takes about two weeks to go all the way through the canyon, and a motorized raft takes about one week.

Rafting the Colorado River provides adventure and beauty visitors can't find anywhere else.

Once the trip starts, there is no way out. On raft trips, rafters take all their food and other supplies with them. They set up camp every night—including tents, a kitchen, and toilets—and pack it all back onto the rafts the next morning.

If doing a whole Grand Canyon raft trip is out of the question, what about a one-day, fifteen-mile raft trip through Glen Canyon? Glen Canyon is just upstream of the Grand Canyon. It doesn't have rapids, but it has beautiful red sandstone cliffs. This trip ends at Lees Ferry, which is where Grand Canyon raft trips begin. There, people inflate their rafts and load them with supplies. Downstream, the river descends and the cliffs rise. That's where the first rapid is.

Only a few miles after starting into the Grand Canyon, the cliffs are hundreds of feet high. After a few days, they'll be thousands of feet high. All the canyon's rock layers emerge one by one. It's like reading a giant stone book page by page. In eight miles, rafters come to the first big rapid, called Badger.

It's a long roller coaster, with waves many feet high. But this isn't an amusement park ride, totally controlled and safe. There is real danger on this river. Some rapids have big boulders that have to be dodged. Some have "holes," spots where the water drops so steeply that it circles back upstream and could trap a raft, at least for a while.

In some rapids, the waves are so big, ten or fifteen feet high, they could flip a raft and toss everyone into the river. It takes a lot of skill and nerve to run this river. All those big waves will not only splash you, they'll drench you.

Colorado River rapids are exciting, but this is no amusement park. They really are dangerous.

As you go through more big rapids, it gets easier to believe that the Colorado River could carve the Grand Canyon. Falling water has a lot of power, especially if it is full of sand and dirt, which makes it like liquid sandpaper scratching the rocks.

Of course, it took a lot of time to cut the canyon, maybe six million years. But the canyon is still a recent event, geologically speaking. Compared to the rocks the canyon reveals, the oldest of which are 1.8 billion years old—300 times older than the canyon—the canyon is a baby.

The river cut the depth of the canyon, but the width was cut by storms. The rain fell into the sides of the canyon and started flash floods that swept boulders and dirt into the river. Gradually, the river eroded those boulders into dirt and hauled the dirt away.

Some of that dirt ended up in the ocean, and some was dropped in the deserts of southern California, creating great soil for growing vegetables. When you eat a hamburger or a salad, the lettuce in it may have grown in soil that was eroded from the Grand Canyon millions of years ago.

To some people, geology can seem an abstract subject, a bunch of ideas that has little

John Wesley Powell lost an arm in the Civil War,
but this didn't stop him from making a dangerous river trip.

connection with daily life. But for John Wesley Powell, geology was so fascinating that he risked his life to be the first person to explore the Grand Canyon by boat.

In 1869, no one knew if a boat could even get through the canyon. Maybe the river held waterfalls or monster whirlpools! Powell needed even more courage because he couldn't swim. He had lost his right arm in the Civil War.

Powell's river journey lasted about 1,000 miles and 100 days, starting on the Green River in Wyoming. He had four wooden boats and nine other men.

Back then, no one knew much about running rapids. Powell's boats weren't the best designs for rapids. They were hard to steer and too easy to roll over. Only two weeks into the trip, one of Powell's boats hit boulders and was smashed apart. Powell and his men lost one-third of their food. They had to learn fast about running rapids.

Two years after his 1869 river expedition,
Powell led a second expedition.

Powell went through one long canyon after another and was amazed by their geology and beauty. He gave them names like Flaming Gorge,

Desolation Canyon, and Labyrinth Canyon. Finally he started into the Grand Canyon.

He wrote: "We are now ready to start our way down the Great Unknown. . . . We are three quarters of a mile in the depths of the earth and the great river shrinks into insignificance. . . . The waves are but puny ripples, and we but pigmies, running up and down the sands or lost among the boulders. We have an unknown distance yet to run, an unknown river to explore. What falls there are, we know not; what rocks beset the channel, we know not."

The Grand Canyon had some of the worst rapids yet. Sometimes Powell's boats were out of control, pushed and filled by giant waves and spun by whirlpools. The men were running out of food, and their clothes and boots were falling apart.

At a bad rapid near the end of the canyon, three men decided they'd had enough. They left the river to head for towns dozens of miles away. They were never seen again. Soon, Powell and his remaining men emerged from the canyon.

Chapter 4
Rafting Today

For rafters, going through the Grand Canyon
is the adventure of a lifetime.

On an oar raft in today's canyon, the guide
may give rafters a chance to row the boat, at least
on a calm stretch of the river. In rapids rafters
can still play an important role. When big waves
hit the raft, it starts to rise or fold up. The rafters
riding in front can lean forward and give the raft
balance. This is called "high siding."

There are lots of types of boats on the river. Some trips have paddle rafts, where people aren't just along for the ride but use paddles to move the raft, including through the rapids. On the back of the paddle raft, a guide calls out instructions and helps steer.

Some trips have inflatable kayaks (also called "duckies") that are like small rafts for one or two people. There are also hard-shelled kayaks that skilled kayakers can roll back up when they get knocked over. There are also wooden boats called dories. They are better designed than Powell's wooden boats, but you still can't afford to hit rocks.

The rapids keep coming, some bigger and some smaller. Hance Rapid drops thirty feet in a quarter of a mile and holds a maze of boulders that rafters have to maneuver around. In the canyon's bottom layer of rocks, the black schist is streaked with pink granite. The river has eroded it into many strange, spooky shapes.

But a river trip offers a lot more than just rapids. There are side canyons every few miles.

An adventurous hiker can find springs, creeks, pools, waterfalls, and very narrow and curving passageways in the cliffs.

Along the river is Vasey's Paradise, a spring that gushes out of the cliffs and waters a big slope of wildflowers. Redwall Cavern, a huge riverside cave with a sandy floor, is as big as a soccer field.

Vasey's Paradise is a very special habitat and is home to an endangered species of snail and other sensitive species.

The ruins of villages where Native Americans lived 1,000 years ago are visible at several places. Their broken pottery is still there. All along the way, wildlife—including blue herons, coyotes, desert bighorn sheep, and ringtails—live.

National Park Service Director Steven Mather (far left)
and Grand Canyon Superintendent Dewitt Raeburn (front right)
pose with friends in front of the Powell Memorial
at the Grand Canyon.

In the seventy-five years after John Wesley Powell's river journey, not many people boated through the Grand Canyon. It was considered too dangerous. A few people went to study geology, and a few went looking for gold or other wealth.

Eventually, people started going for the sheer adventure of it. In 1937, Buzz Holmstrom made the first solo trip through the canyon. In 1938, Norm Nevills starting taking paying passengers down the river in wooden boats.

Nevills's first customers were two botanists, Lois Jotter and Elzada Clover, who wanted to study Grand Canyon plants. They also became the first women to go through the entire canyon. In 1952, a daring woman named Georgie White started using rubber rafts to carry passengers.

The beautiful blue-green color of the water at Havasu Falls is created by calcium carobate in the water.

In the thirty miles after Hance Rapid, the river passes Phantom Ranch and the Bright Angel Trail and forms some of the worst rapids in the canyon.

In Granite Rapid, the river brushes against a cliff, and the waves bouncing off it are very chaotic. In Hermit Rapid, the waves can be fifteen feet tall. Crystal Rapid was fairly mild until a 1966 flash flood swept hundreds of tons of boulders into the river.

Deer Creek has a big waterfall right beside the river. From there, a trail leads up to a natural rock plaza with pools and ancient Native American pictographs.

The rapids at Lava Falls are the most difficult rapids in the Grand Canyon and can be the most scary and exhilarating part of any rafting trip.

Havasu has a long series of waterfalls and pools with beautiful blue-green water. Eight miles up the creek is the village of the Havasupai, Native Americans who have lived and farmed there for centuries.

At mile 179, there are cliffs formed when lava flowed into the canyon long ago from volcanoes on the rim. The lava formed a rapid called Lava Falls, one of the most famous rapids in the world. Even experienced river guides get nervous about Lava Falls, for it is very steep, powerful, and chaotic.

River guides enjoy testing their skills against the river, but they don't really enjoy testing their dumb luck against the river. In Lava Falls there's a bit too much chance involved. Guides stop above the rapid and walk up to a ledge that gives them a good look at the rapid.

It is important to enter the rapid at exactly the right place. But Lava Falls is so steep that, once the guides are back in the raft, even they can have a hard time recognizing where they are. Even experienced guides have gotten confused and plunged into the worst part of the chaos.

Chapter 5
Wildlife

Mountain lions are called by different names in different areas. At the Grand Canyon, they are called mountain lions, but other names include cougar, puma, panther, and catamount.

Many people go to national parks mainly to see wildlife. Though Yellowstone National Park has amazing geological wonders like geysers, many people have more fun seeing its bison and bears.

National parks preserve nature as it was long ago. Before human cities filled the land, wild plants and animals had a lot more space to live. Some national parks were created for the sake of their biological wonders—Sequoia for its giant trees, the Everglades for its swamps.

The Grand Canyon may be the world's most famous display of rocks, but it also has some amazing animals and plants. Because national parks don't allow hunting, the animals there are not too shy and will often let people get a good look at them.

Driving the road between Grand Canyon Village and Desert View, you may notice a yellow highway warning sign. It is seldom seen anywhere else and has a running animal on it. In the West, this animal is called a mountain lion. In other parts of the country, it is often called a cougar. This is a mountain lion crossing zone.

Mountain Lion Crossing signs warn visitors about local mountain lions to try to prevent car strikes.

Drivers probably won't see any mountain lions, for there aren't many in the park and they only come out at night. Like a housecat, mountain lions are amazing jumpers and hunters. They can climb a tree or cliff, wait for an elk or deer to come along, and jump on the elk or deer, and knock it over. Fortunately, mountain lions are afraid of people and don't bother them.

Bighorn Sheep are social animals and typically live in small herds of males and females together.

From nearby mountains, black bears sometimes wander to the South Rim looking for a place to live. But the rim forests don't have enough of the food bears need, like juicy berries, so the bears usually don't hang around for long.

Inside the canyon live desert bighorn sheep. The males have curving horns. Visitors hardly ever see desert bighorn sheep on the rim. The sheep feel safer on cliffs, where their sharp hoofs can hook into tiny rock ledges, letting them bound up or down the cliffs. If mountain lions try to catch them, they usually get away.

Coyotes are very smart animals, which allows them to live both in the forests on the canyon rim and in the deserts at the canyon bottom. Unlike wolves, which live in packs, coyotes are more solitary. The park also has gray foxes, the only member of the dog family that can climb trees.

Mule deer are specially adapted to dry, hot environments. Their ears help radiate heat and keep their bodies cooler.

The deer in this part of the country are called mule deer because their ears look like the ears of mules. Mule deer can point each ear in a different direction. Mule deer are adapted for a dry climate, where it may not rain for two months and there are few creeks or lakes. They can get moisture right out of their food.

Visitors have a good chance of seeing elk, which can weigh up to 750 pounds. Their antlers can weigh up to fifty pounds. They shed their antlers in the spring and grow new ones at a rate of about half an inch per day.

The elk are accustomed to cars and people and they'll stand right by the roads and let people look at them. You can't have this experience in a zoo, where the animals are in cages. But don't forget: these are still wild animals, and they don't like people to get too close. They can be unpredictable and dangerous. Some careless park visitors have gotten hurt.

What's the most dangerous animal in the park? Elk? Or rattlesnakes? Or scorpions? Or tarantulas? The most dangerous animal is actually a cute little squirrel.

They are called rock squirrels because they live on the ground and not in trees. They come up to visitors and beg for food. But almost every day, a squirrel bites someone, usually a kid. Sometimes it's an accident, but sometimes kids are teasing the squirrels. These squirrels can carry diseases, so everyone that gets bitten needs to see a doctor and maybe get shots, which is not a fun way to spend a vacation.

What's the most dangerous animal in the park?
This cute rock squirrel.

Another reason not to feed the wildlife is because most of the food people give them is not good for them and can make them sick.

The rim does have tarantulas, and in the autumn months visitors may see them wandering around on the sidewalks. Hollywood movies have given tarantulas a bad reputation, but they really aren't dangerous.

The rim doesn't have any rattlesnakes or scorpions because they need a warmer climate. They live in the desert inside the canyon. In a desert, food is hard to find, so plants defend themselves with sharp needles, and animals protect themselves with venom.

For both rattlesnakes and scorpions, their venom is mainly for hunting food, small things like bugs and mice. They don't want to waste their venom on big animals like humans, and they won't bother people unless they think people are attacking them. Hardly anyone has been bitten by a rattlesnake in the Grand Canyon.

Scorpions can be avoided by obeying a few rules. Scorpions like to hide in tight places like cracks in rocks or logs, so visitors shouldn't stick their fingers in there. If people are camping, they should keep their tents zipped up. If they leave their boots outside, they should shake them out in the morning.

The Grand Canyon Pink Rattlesnake is only found in the Grand Canyon, and is one of very few pink rattlesnakes!

The birds most likely to be seen at the canyon are ravens. Ravens are cousins to crows, but bigger and with larger beaks. Ravens are one of the smartest birds in the world, which allows them to survive in the harshest environmnets. They can survive in areas of arctic-like cold to desert-hot. Ravens love to fly for the fun of it, and are very acrobatic.

If you are lucky, you may spot a California condor, the largest bird in North America. It has a wingspan of nearly ten feet. In the 1980s the California condor was nearly extinct, its total population down to only twenty-two. Wildlife biologists have helped the population recover to many hundreds.

The California condor is one of the rarest birds in the world.

Some condors live and raise families in caves inside the Grand Canyon. At a distance, condors can be hard to tell apart from turkey vultures. The best way to tell is that condors fly with their wings spread out, while turkey vultures hold their wings in a "V" shape and rock back and forth.

The canyon also has golden eagles, peregrine falcons, and red-tailed hawks. The smaller birds that are zipping around really fast are probably swallows or swifts. A blue bird, the pinyon jay, lives off the nuts of the pinyon pine tree.

Most of the trees on the South Rim are of three types: pinyon pine trees, juniper trees, and ponderosa pine trees. The pinyon pine tree has nuts that are incredibly nutritious. Native Americans often relied on pine nuts to get them through the winter. In the fall, when the nuts are ripe, you can pick them off the ground and taste them.

Be careful! When they are still in their shells, pine nuts look a lot like deer poop! A guidebook can help people recognize different kinds of animal poop and tracks. You don't want to eat the wrong thing!

Juniper trees have blue-green berries, but these berries are not soft and juicy like you'd expect from the word "berry." Juniper berries are hard nuggets and have a bitter taste, so many birds and animals won't eat them.

Ponderosa pine, pinyon pine, and juniper trees are the three most common trees at the rim of the Grand Canyon.

The ponderosa pine tree is straight and tall, and the older ones are orange colored. The bark of ponderosa trees has a scent that reminds some people of vanilla and others of butterscotch.

All three of these trees are evergreens. That means they don't have leaves that turn colors and fall off in autumn, but needles that stay green all winter. On the North Rim, which is 1,000 feet higher than the South Rim and thus cooler and wetter, there are spruce, fir, and white-barked aspen trees.

Inside the canyon are desert plants, including lots of cacti. They may be painful to touch, but their flowers can be beautiful to look at. Cacti have thick skin to protect themselves from drying out in the sun. Lizards do too. Lizards spend much of the day hiding in shadows, which proves they may be smarter than the humans walking around in the summer heat.

Some Cacti live at all levels of the Grand Canyon,
but they are much more common closer to the canyon floor.

Chapter 6
Native Americans

A thousand years ago Native Americans lived inside the Grand Canyon and along the rim. They were farmers, growing mainly corn, beans, and squash, which offered a balanced diet. Their corn was a lot smaller than the Midwestern corn in grocery stores today, but it was well adapted for a dry climate.

This wasn't an easy place to farm. The soil wasn't great and the rain wasn't generous. But the canyon, with different climates between the rim and the bottom, allowed these Native Americans to do something other farmers could not. They could spend summers farming on the rim and spend winters at the canyon bottom, growing a second crop.

Rain was very important, so it played a central role in their art and religion. Because they lived in the same places for many years, they put a lot of effort into building sturdy stone houses, called pueblos. That is why these people are called "Puebloans."

The Cliff Palace ruins at nearby Mesa Verde National Park is an example of a pueblo settlement.

The ruins of these villages are still there today, and visitors can walk through them. On the South Rim is Tusayan Ruin, which includes a kiva (an underground church) and a small museum. On the North Rim is a ruin called Walhalla Glades. You don't have to believe in ghosts to feel the presence of the people who lived there.

Puebloan kids would help out with the crops. Because crops attract hungry animals like rabbits and deer, they might need to guard the crops with a bow and arrow. That could also add some meat to their meals.

Villages could be a long way from water, so the children might have to carry water in beautifully-painted clay pots. Sometimes they would hike into the canyon to visit relatives who lived there, or to search for wild plants they couldn't find on the rim.

Puebloan kids learned a lot of tribal knowledge from their parents and grandparents. They learned how to make medicine, food, clothing, sandals, rope, and all kinds of necessary things. At night, people would tell stories about the stars, their ancestors, old heroes, or the gods. At the right times, people would perform ceremonies to celebrate the rain, the crops, and being alive.

Today, twenty Puebloan tribes live
in New Mexico and Arizona.

The Grand Canyon Puebloans were part
of a larger culture that stretched hundreds of
miles. The Puebloans built cities like Mesa Verde
(which today is a national park). But then a long
drought made farming impossible in most of
the Southwest.

The Puebloans abandoned most of their
villages and retreated to places with more reliable
water. The Puebloans still live in those places.
The tribes are the Hopi and Zuni and the tribes
of the Rio Grande River in New Mexico.

Today their houses, kivas, pottery, and religion are similar to what they were long ago. In the Hopi and Zuni creation stories, the Grand Canyon is where the human race emerged into this world. The Hopis and Zunis still make religious pilgrimages into the canyon.

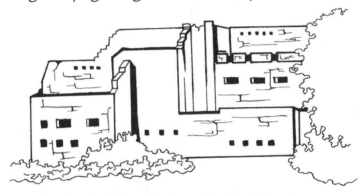

Designed to look like a Hopi pueblo, Hopi House was many park visitors' first encounter with non-European architecture.

On the South Rim you can also go into two buildings that were inspired by the Hopis. These buildings were designed by architect Mary Colter, who admired the Hopis for their long and deep connections with the Grand Canyon. Her Hopi House is a three-story pueblo, just like the stone houses in which the Hopis live. It is a shop for Native American pottery, jewelry, rugs, and katsina dolls.

The Watchtower overlooks the Painted Desert. Visitors can see more than 100 miles away on a clear day.

Her Desert View Watchtower is a seventy-foot-tall tower, like towers at Mesa Verde. Her tower is full of murals that depict Hopi life and legends and what the Grand Canyon means to them. Narrow staircases climb to the top of the tower and give great views of the canyon.

After the Puebloans left the Grand Canyon region, other peoples moved in. From the north came the Navajos—their own word for themselves is "Diné." They didn't have to rely on farming, as they lived by hunting animals and gathering wild plants.

The Navajos soon adopted a new way of life: sheep grazing. Navajo kids herd the sheep with help from their energetic and smart sheepdogs. With lots of sheep, the Navajos also have lots of wool, and they weave it into high-quality, world-famous rugs. People will pay thousands of dollars for a Navajo rug, which they place not on the floor but on the wall as art.

The Navajos are also famous for making jewelry featuring a blue mineral called turquoise. To Navajos, turquoise symbolizes water, always a precious thing for desert people.

When approaching or leaving the Grand Canyon at its eastern entrance at Desert View, people are driving across Navajo land. Visitors may see their traditional homes, called hogans, which have eight sides and a door that always faces east, the direction of the rising sun.

Navajos mix together the modern world, like pickup trucks, with ancient traditions, like medicine men and elaborate healing ceremonies. During World War II, the US Marines recruited hundreds of Navajos. They used their language as a secret code to send messages during battles in the Pacific Ocean. The Navajo code talkers helped win the war.

Today, the Navajos are the largest tribe in America, with the largest reservation. Most tribes were forced off their original homelands. But the Navajos and Hopis are still living on the same lands where they were many centuries ago. Navajos and Hopis feel deep, sacred bonds with their lands.

While the Navajos were moving into the Grand Canyon area from the north, other people were moving in from the west. They were called the Hualapai and the Paiutes.

One group of Hualapai settled in a side canyon of the Grand Canyon that had a creek and good soil. These people became farmers and eventually defined themselves as a separate people, the Havasupai.

Today, many visitors hike eight miles into Havasu Canyon to camp and enjoy the waterfalls

Built on the Hualapai Indian Reservation, the Skywalk reaches seventy feet out into the Grand Canyon.

and pools, which make great swimming pools. For Havasupai kids, this is home.

Farther west, the Hualapai run raft trips at the tail end of the Grand Canyon. On the rim, they built the Skywalk, a glass horseshoe that sticks out over the canyon. The Paiutes live on the other, north side of the canyon. For them too, the canyon holds sacred places and meaning.

Chapter 7
Pioneers

For centuries after the Hopis left the Grand Canyon, they lived in modest stone villages, grew corn, and performed ceremonies of thanks for rain and life. Then one day, some strangers showed up. They had different values and were seeking gold and empire. These were the Spanish conquistadors, the first Europeans to explore the Southwest.

The year was 1540, less than fifty years after Columbus landed in America. Americans tend to write the country's history from an English point of view. They say American history started in 1620 when the pilgrims landed at Plymouth Rock.

Eighty years before that, the Spanish were exploring the West. The Spanish brought a lot of trouble to Native Americans, but also some helpful things like horses.

The first Europeans to see the Grand Canyon were
Spanish conquistadores searching
for El Dorado or Cibola, the City of Gold.

When the Spanish saw the Grand Canyon, they had a hard time figuring it out. They looked at the Colorado River and thought it was a creek maybe six feet wide. It is actually about 300 feet across, the length of a football field.

The Spanish tried to hike into the canyon but soon realized it was much bigger than they thought. The Spanish considered the canyon to be nothing but an obstacle and took little further interest in it.

As the United States expanded westward, Americans began seeing the Grand Canyon. But they weren't interested in the canyon as a beautiful natural wonder, only as a source of riches. In the 1820s, fur trappers, searching for beaver along the Colorado River, entered the canyon.

In 1857, Lieutenant Joseph Ives of the US Army tested the Colorado River as a transportation route. He captained a primitive steamboat up the river from its mouth. Ives wrecked his boat long before reaching the Grand Canyon, and he declared that the canyon was "altogether valueless."

In the 1880s, prospectors combed the Grand Canyon for mineral wealth, but few prospectors made any profit.

In the 1880s, prospectors began combing the canyon for minerals. In 1889, railroad surveyor Robert Stanton wanted to build a railroad through the entire canyon, even if he had to blast away the cliffs.

The canyon held little gold or silver, but it did have some copper, which was valuable as wiring in the new age of electricity. Still, mining inside the canyon took a great deal of trouble and expense.

Miners had to build a trail to the mine and run a team of mules to haul out ore. When they got to the rim, the railroad was still fifty miles away. Only a half dozen Grand Canyon mines ever made much of a profit.

This quest for riches was a big contrast with John Wesley Powell, who explored from a love of nature and scientific curiosity. A few years after his river expedition, Powell brought an artist, Thomas Moran, to the canyon. Moran painted a giant picture which was hung in the US Capitol building. Americans began realizing that the canyon was a unique natural wonder.

Thomas Moran attempted to capture the beauty
of future national parks, like Yellowstone, through art.

In the 1880s, tourists started going to the canyon. They paid miners for food, camping, and mule rides down their trails. Soon, miners were making more money from tourists than from mining. They set up tourist camps of tents and log cabins.

The first white American to settle at the Grand Canyon was John Hance. Around his campfires, he enjoyed telling tall tales about the Grand Canyon. Here's one:

On a dare, John Hance once tried to jump his horse Darby across the canyon. But when they were only halfway across, Darby ran out of momentum and began to fall. It was 5,000 feet to the bottom. But John, still sitting on Darby, wasn't worried. When Darby was only two feet from hitting bottom, John yelled "Whoa!" John had trained Darby so well, Darby stopped. John stepped safely onto the ground.

One visitor to the park claimed, "To see the canyon only and not to see Captain John Hance is to miss half the show."

The first Americans to raise a family at the canyon were William and Ada Bass. In the 1880s William Bass was a train dispatcher in New York City, but this was a stressful job and he had a nervous breakdown. Wanting to get far away from city life, he found the Grand Canyon and went prospecting. He started some mines, and then started taking tourists down his trail.

The Bass family's children helped their parents lead tours and take care of the trail.

One day a twenty-seven-year-old woman named Ada came to see the canyon. She was well-educated and a music teacher. William's life was much rougher, but he played the violin, wrote poetry, loved astronomy, and had mastered the amazing Grand Canyon. Soon Ada and William got married. They had four children. But Ada's life was hard.

They didn't have a reliable water supply. Sometimes to do the laundry Ada had to pack it onto a mule and take it eight miles down their trail to the Colorado River. The river was often too muddy to get clothes really clean. Then she packed the clothes back onto the mule and climbed nearly 5,000 feet to get home.

It was hard enough taking care of her own family, but she also had to cook for all their tourists. At least Ada had a piano to enjoy.

John Hance and William and Ada Bass never made much money from the canyon, but they had fallen in love with it. They wanted to stay there, whatever it took. The Grand Canyon has always attracted strong and unusual characters with a love of adventure and beauty.

In 1901 the Santa Fe Railway arrived at the South Rim and started bringing lots of tourists. It also brought a new cast of strong and unusual characters.

In 1901 the first train arrived at the Grand Canyon
and made it a popular tourist destination.

Mary Colter was a thirty-five-year-old high school teacher in St. Paul, Minnesota. Then the Santa Fe Railway asked her to design a building at the Grand Canyon. Mary hadn't been to architecture school—very few women could get into architecture school in that era.

Colter did have a keen eye for Native American art. The Santa Fe Railway's business partner was the Fred Harvey Company. They built and managed all the Santa Fe Railway's hotels and restaurants. They wanted some Native American designs for the tourist facilities they were building in the Southwest.

Mary's first building was Hopi House, which really did have Hopis living upstairs. They showed tourists how they made pottery and jewelry and performed dances outside.

Mary wanted Hopi House to be realistic, so she made its doorways kind of short, just like in real Hopi homes. This meant that most tourists would bump their heads unless they bent over.

At first, the Fred Harvey Company wasn't sure whether Mary was crazy or brilliant. They decided she was a genius and kept her working for them for fifty years. At the Grand Canyon, Mary designed eight buildings or sets of buildings.

Her Lookout Studio had a geological inspiration and blends into the cliffs. Her Bright Angel Lodge and Hermits Rest had pioneer inspirations.

Colter had a big influence on the kind of architecture found in many national parks today. The buildings emphasize natural materials like stone and wood and woodsy colors like green and brown.

The Fred Harvey Company was famous for its waitresses, called "Harvey Girls." They were mostly from the East and Midwest, but they had a great sense of adventure and used their jobs to explore the West. In 1946, Judy Garland, who played Dorothy in *The Wizard of OZ*, starred in the movie musical *The Harvey Girls*.

Chapter 8
Preserving the View

In 1902, two brothers, Ellsworth and Emery
Kolb, came to the canyon in search of adventure.
Ellsworth was twenty-five years old, and Emery

The older Kolb brother, Ellsworth, saw the beauty of the
Grand Canyon as a bellhop for the Bright Angel Hotel. He soon
told his younger brother, Emery, to join him at the canyon.

twenty-one. To stay at the canyon, they went into the photography business.

Photography was still a new and exotic technology. They built a small photo studio at the top of the Bright Angel Trail and continued expanding it for years, turning it into a nice house.

The mule rides are so popular that visitors have to reserve their spot over a year in advance!

They took photos of mule riders as they headed down the trail. They sold the photos when the riders returned. Some of these rides were one-day trips, so the Kolbs had to be quick about developing their photos. This took water, and water could be in short supply on the rim.

Sometimes the Kolbs had to put their big glass negatives into a backpack. They would then hike four and a half miles down the trail to Indian Garden, where they built a darkroom. Then they had to race back up the trail to beat the mule riders to the top, a nine-mile roundtrip.

Tourists can still visit Kolb Studio, which is now an art gallery and bookstore operated by the Grand Canyon Association.

The Kolbs hiked all over the canyon and discovered and photographed amazing places, like waterfalls and natural rock arches. They enjoyed taking photos of themselves and others in dangerous situations, such as dangling by rope over a cliff.

In 1911, the Kolbs built boats and repeated John Wesley Powell's journey down the Green and Colorado rivers. They took a movie camera and filmed their adventure, which had plenty of drama and mishaps.

They added an auditorium onto their studio and showed their movie there for the next sixty years. That made it the longest running movie in world history. The Kolb Studio is still there today, perched right on the edge of the canyon.

In 1903, another kind of pioneer came to the Grand Canyon, a pioneer conservationist, President Theodore Roosevelt. He was known by his nickname "Teddy," and he was the inspiration for the teddy bear.

Teddy Roosevelt grew up in the glory days of the Wild West and he loved the idea of Americans heroically conquering the frontier. As a young man, he went to the Dakotas and hunted bison and elk. But he saw that America's once-great bison herds were almost gone, and he saw Americans wasting topsoil and other valuable resources.

He realized that America's frontier wouldn't last forever and that we had to change some of our wasteful habits. He saw that we needed to protect our greatest natural wonders, like the Grand Canyon, before they were ruined. As president he pushed to create many national parks.

President Theodore Roosevelt declared the Grand Canyon a National Monument in 1908. In 1919, President Woodrow Wilson further protected it by making it a National Park.

Roosevelt loved the Grand Canyon. In his 1903 visit he declared: "Leave it as it is....The ages have been at work on it, and man can only mar it." In 1908, Roosevelt protected the Grand Canyon by making it a national monument. He wanted the canyon to be a national park, but this required an act of Congress.

Many Arizonans and Americans felt that private lands and profits were more important than national parks. It would be 1919 before the Grand Canyon became a national park, nearly fifty years after Yellowstone became the first.

Chapter 9
Getting There is Part of the Fun

If you had wanted to visit the Grand Canyon in the days of the Wild West, you would have needed to ride a horse or a stagecoach for at least fifty miles from the nearest towns.

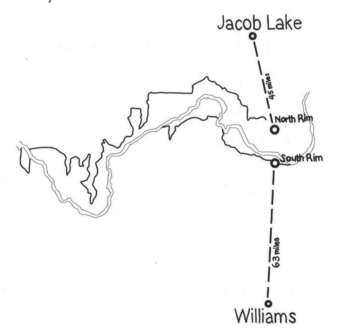

Before the trains, visitors had to travel to the canyon from nearby towns on horses or in horse-drawn carriages or stagecoaches. It was not a pleasant journey.

The roads were dirt, very dusty and sometimes muddy, and always bumpy. It would take all day to get to the canyon, and the lodging there was primitive. Not many people went.

After 1901, visitors could take a train with a steam locomotive to the canyon. The Santa Fe Railway built a spur line from the town of Williams to the canyon. They also built nice hotels and restaurants and other buildings.

Yet as the decades passed, Americans preferred traveling by car and plane. In the 1960s the Santa Fe Railway abandoned its Grand Canyon train.

About twenty-five years later, some train lovers rebuilt the canyon railroad. The old Santa Fe Railway equipment and tracks and bridges were long gone, so the builders had to start from scratch.

Today, a train (with a diesel locomotive) comes up to the canyon every day. The National Park Service likes the train because the people who ride the train don't need somewhere to park.

The current Grand Canyon Railway features cowboys, bandits, and western musicians on the restored rail cars.

This means hundreds of people aren't driving to the park and looking for parking places. Kids like the train because this is the first time many have ridden on a train.

Along the way, the train goes through beautiful forests. The train company likes to put on a show, so it's not a surprise if some Wild West bandits on horses try to rob the train. This is the only train in America that actually stops for robbers and lets them get on board! In December, the train becomes a Polar Express.

Another kind of "train" will take visitors to the bottom of the canyon—a train of mules. Grand Canyon mules are world famous. Their clip-clopping feet were portrayed in a popular piece of classical music, Ferde Grofé's "Grand Canyon Suite." Mules have been carrying people into the canyon every day for more than 100 years, and they've never killed anyone.

The park uses mules instead of horses because mules can see their feet better than horses can. When you are on a narrow trail on the edge of a cliff, you want an animal that always knows exactly where all four of its feet are.

Mules are also sturdy animals that can do very hard work in hard conditions, such as the canyon's summer heat. In the winter mules get "snow tires," horseshoes with cleats for gripping any snow on the trail.

Visitors have to plan far ahead to get a mule ride, since the waiting list can be two years long. Riders also need to be at least nine years old and four feet, nine inches tall. If they aren't that tall, they can't reach the stirrups.

The ride starts early in the morning, which lets riders beat the summer heat. The ride is led by experienced cowboys and cowgirls. At a corral at the top of the Bright Angel Trail, they will line up the mules and pick the best one for each rider.

If the cowboy senses that a rider is nervous, he may crack a joke, like this: "I'll bet you've never ridden a mule or horse before, have you? Well, we've got the perfect mule for you. You've never ridden a mule before, and this mule has never been ridden by anyone before, and it's never been into the canyon before."

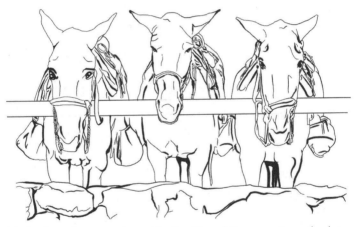

Mules have been preferred in the Grand Canyon since the late 1800s when John Hance began taking tourists down on mules.

Off they go, bouncing along. It makes some people nervous that the mules like to walk right on the edge of the cliff. After nearly five hours, the mule train crosses the bridge over the Colorado River and arrives at Phantom Ranch.

In the morning, they'll head back up. By the time the ride is done, riders may be sore, but they'll be sore in a different location than the hikers, who have sore feet.

If visitors don't bring their own bicycle to the park, they can rent one at a bicycle shop next to the Visitor Center. From there, it's a mile and a half ride through the forest to the canyon rim. Then they can ride along the rim for about a mile.

Paved trails follow the rim for many miles (with only modest slopes), but most of them are closed to bikes since there are too many people on them. To explore the rest of the rim trails visitors have to go for a walk.

Another place they can ride a bike is the Hermit Road, a seven-mile rim road that is closed to cars for most of the year.

In many national parks cars have become a problem, because there are too many. In the

1970s, Grand Canyon National Park addressed this problem by starting a free bus system.

There are three different typs of forest at the Grand Canyon: forests of pinyon pin and juniper trees, forests of pondersoa pines, and forests of spruce and fir trees.

The Hermit Road bus stops at nine places to enjoy great views. Some of the stops are near steep cliffs, the Colorado River, famous rapids, a monument to John Wesley Powell, and an abandoned mine.

At the end of the Hermit Road is Hermits Rest, a cave-like gift shop and snack bar, designed by architect Mary Colter.

Another way to see the canyon is to fly over it in a sightseeing helicopter or small airplane. These trips start at the airport just outside the park. It's a very dramatic ride, especially the moment when the plane is flying over the rim forests and suddenly the whole canyon appears beneath it.

Helicopter trips above the canyon offer beautiful views, but only National Park Service helicopters are allowed to fly beneath the rim.

If a helicopter ride isn't mind-boggling enough, how about taking a spaceship to the stars? Grand Canyon National Park has those too.

These spaceships are called telescopes. In the warmer months, park rangers often set up telescopes near the Visitor Center. They let visitors get a close look at the moon's craters and Saturn's rings. They show visitors a nebula's colorful clouds of gas and a distant galaxy's billions of stars.

With a laser pointer, the ranger will point out the constellations, the planets, and some interesting stars. Stargazers don't need any help to spot the Milky Way, a belt of light that stretches across the whole sky. That is our own galaxy, viewed from the inside.

These days, most kids grow up in cities or suburbs with lots of artificial lights that block the view of the night sky. But Grand Canyon National Park is a long way from city lights, and it has a high elevation and dry air. All are good for getting a clear view of the Milky Way and the rest of the night sky.

National parks are supposed to show people the wonders of nature, and that includes the night sky. Every summer, the park offers a "Star Party," with dozens of amateur astronomers bringing telescopes and letting visitors look through them.

Commonly viewed objects at star parties are our moon and Saturn, with its colorful rings.

Chapter 10
You Can be a Park Ranger

Many people travel a long way and spend a lot of money to enjoy a day or two at Grand Canyon National Park. They find the canyon inspiring and take home good memories and photographs.

They go back to their jobs or schools in a busy city, and they wish they could have spent more time at the Grand Canyon or other national parks.

There is one job that lets you live in a national park all year long. You could watch a canyon sunset any day of the week. You could walk your dog on the sidewalks along the canyon rim. You could get your exercise by walking down a trail into the canyon. You could be there at just the right moment to see a fantastic rainbow or a desert bighorn sheep.

This job is being a park ranger. Rangers are the people who take care of national parks and park visitors. Some rangers live and work at the

Grand Canyon for twenty or thirty years. They live in houses and apartments not far from the canyon rim.

Many rangers have children who grow up in the park. The South Rim has a school that goes from kindergarten to high school. The classes are small, with about a dozen kids in a grade, but they manage to put together teams for basketball, soccer, baseball, and track.

Their school mascot is "the Phantoms," named for Phantom Ranch. Grand Canyon Village is a town just like any other small town, with its own grocery store, churches, a bank, and a small hospital.

Rangers wear a uniform that evolved from the uniforms of the US Cavalry, which protected the first national parks. Ranger uniforms include boots, a flat brown hat, and a golden badge.

The rangers that visitors are most likely to meet are called "interpretative" rangers, which means they help visitors understand the park. They lead walks along the rim and tell stories about the canyon, its wildlife, and people who lived here in the past.

The rangers at the Grand Canyon answer questions about everything from fossils, plants, and animals to geology, history, and astronomy.

In the evening, at an outdoor theater with a campfire and a giant screen for showing pictures, they give hour-long talks about their favorite subjects. In the winter these talks are given at an indoor theater. At the Visitor Center, rangers answer questions and help visitors plan their day.

Other kinds of rangers do other jobs:

Wildlife biologists study the animals in the park. For example, some set up cameras to watch mountain lions sneaking around.

The visitor center is usually the first stop for tourists as they plan their day exploring the Grand Canyon.

Archaeologists find, study, and protect ancient Native American ruins.

Botanists study and protect trees, bushes, and wildflowers.

Backcountry rangers patrol the hiking trails inside the canyon and help hikers who are hurt or worn out.

River rangers raft down the Colorado River and take care of rafters and campsites.

Law enforcement rangers keep an eye on people who bring their bad habits to the park. This includes people who litter, cause car wrecks, or are too loud while other visitors are trying to enjoy the sounds of nature.

Trail crew rangers rebuild the canyon's trails, which are always wearing down from human and mule feet and from rainstorms.

Maintenance rangers keep everything in the park working properly, including roads and buildings.

Eddie McKee became the Grand Canyon's naturalist after falling in love with the park during a summer internship.

Eddie McKee was a ranger in the 1930s. He loved hiking and roamed far to study the canyon's geology and wildlife, and he made many new discoveries.

One day on a canyon trail, he spotted an unknown species of rattlesnake. He didn't have a tool or container for capturing it, so he grabbed it behind the head and carried it out of the canyon. Then he drove home with one hand on the steering wheel while his other hand held the snake out the window. Don't try that at home!

One summer, Eddie met Barbara, a lady biologist, doing research on the North Rim. To date her, he hiked across the canyon, more than forty miles round-trip. Barbara was impressed, and they got married.

Another ranger was Bruce Aiken, who lived inside the canyon at Roaring Springs for thirty years. He ran the pumps that supply water to both rims.

He and his wife Mary raised three kids there, home schooling them. They had a nice little house beside the trail that runs from the North Rim to Phantom Ranch. The kids ran a lemonade stand that was very popular with thirsty hikers. Bruce was an artist, and he lived there so he could paint the Grand Canyon.

Junior Rangers can earn three different badges at Grand Canyon National Park by visiting the North Rim, South Rim, and Phantom Ranch and completing activities.

Kids can become park rangers too, at least honorary ones. National parks have a program called Junior Ranger. It lets kids get more involved with the Grand Canyon. They start by getting an activity book that is full of puzzles, games, codes, lists, and things to draw.

Junior Rangers have to do a few things to qualify. Options include attending a ranger talk, wildlife spotting, or shooting a thirty-second video about their park visit. Then a park ranger will swear them in and give them a Junior Ranger badge and certificate.

Chapter 11
This Land is Your Land

People today are able to visit and enjoy the Grand Canyon because people in the past cared about it. They worked hard to protect it as a national park. If the Grand Canyon wasn't a national park, the entire rim might consist of miles of mansions with gates and security guards to keep tourists away.

If valuable minerals had been discovered in the canyon, the canyon might have been torn apart. It would have had giant strip mines and smoky factories on the rim. In the 1960s the U.S. Congress nearly voted to build two dams inside the canyon. That would have flooded much of the canyon and put an end to river trips. Before the canyon was a national park, visitors had to pay a toll to go down the Bright Angel Trail, which was privately owned.

It's only because the canyon is a national park, where hunting is not allowed, that people have a good chance of seeing wildlife.

Upstream from the Grand Canyon, the Glen Canyon Dam
regulates the flow of the Colorado River
and sparks many environmental debates.

The national parks belong to everyone. Even those who have never been to a national park can enjoy knowing that some of the world's most amazing places belong to them. National parks represent the best of America's democratic ideals.

Politicians have risen above politics to support national parks. The Grand Canyon was made a national monument by a Republican president,

Woodrow Wilson made the Grand Canyon
the fifteenth national park.

Teddy Roosevelt. It was made a national park by
a Democrat president, Woodrow Wilson.

Americans invented the idea of national
parks, and about 150 nations have been inspired

to create their own. When people visit Grand Canyon National Park, they notice that many people have traveled from overseas to visit it.

National parks also mean that people are seeing nature the way it was a hundred years ago, or maybe a million years ago. Natural wonders are not just pretty to look at. They remind us that there is a lot more to the world than human cities and human activities.

Grand Canyon National Park is in Arizona
and follows the path of the canyon and Colorado River.

National parks have two goals. One is to protect natural wonders. The other is to make them accessible to visitors. Sometimes these two goals are hard to combine. If too many cars are coming to national parks, should the park bulldoze forests and wildlife habitats to make more parking lots? Grand Canyon National Park tried to solve this problem by using shuttle buses.

Inside the canyon there aren't enough camping spots, so the park had to limit the numbers of hikers and river runners who can go there.

National parks aren't permanent. They will be here only as long as people care about them. It isn't just politicians and park managers who need to care—it's you too. You care by visiting parks, and by treating them with respect. You don't go to a national park to see someone else's garbage on the ground.

If visitors are enjoying seeing pretty rocks and wildflowers, it's only because for 100 years other visitors have left them there, not taken them home. Visitors should leave only footprints, and take only photos and wonderful memories.

The Grand Canyon National Park welcome sign welcomed
over six million visitors in 2017,
and will welcome many more to come.

After people visit Grand Canyon National Park, they realize that it holds plenty more adventures, enough to keep them coming back for years. It's time to start planning the next trip to the Grand Canyon.

Select Quotes

"Nearly everybody, on taking a first look into the Grand Canyon, comes right out and admits its wonders are absolutely indescribable—and then proceeds to write anywhere from two thousand to fifty thousand words, giving the full details....I do not know anybody who has yet succeed in getting away with the job."

—Irving S. Cobb. "Roughing it Deluxe." *The Saturday Evening Post,* June 7, 1913.

"Each man sees himself in the Grand Canyon—Each one makes his own Canyon before he comes, each one brings and carries away his own Canyon."

—Carl Sandburg. From "Many Hats," *The Complete Poems of Carl Sandburg.* New York: Harcourt Brace Jovanovich, 1970, page 434.

"It seems a gigantic statement for even nature to make....A grand geological library—a collection of stone books....With what wonderful scriptures are their pages filled....carrying us back into the midst of the life of a past infinitely remote. And as we go on and on, studying this old, old life in the light of the life beating warmly about us, we enrich and lengthen our own."

—John Muir. "*The* Grand Canyon of the Colorado." *Century Illustrated Monthly Magazine,* November 1902, 107-16.

"If future generations are to remember us more with gratitude than with sorrow, we must achieve more than just the miracles of technology. We must also leave them a glimpse of the world as God really made it, not just as it looked when we got through with it."

—President Lyndon Johnson. Speech on Sept. 21, 1965

Grand Canyon Timeline

1.8 billion years ago.   Oldest rocks in Grand Canyon are formed

270 million years ago.   Kaibab limestone, top layer of Grand Canyon, is formed

80 million years ago.   Tectonic forces have lifted Grand Canyon rocks out of the sea

6 million years ago.   Colorado River has carved Grand Canyon

12,000 years ago.   Humans have arrived at Grand Canyon

1500   Navajos, Hualapai and Paiutes have moved into Grand Canyon region

1540   Spanish are first Europeans to see Grand Canyon

1869   John Wesley Powell leads first river expedition through Grand Canyon

1893   President Benjamin Harrison makes Grand Canyon a forest preserve (an earlier version of a national forest)

1901   Santa Fe Railway arrives at Grand Canyon

1905   Santa Fe Railway opens El Tovar Hotel and Hopi House

1908   President Theodore Roosevelt makes Grand Canyon a national monument

1919   Grand Canyon becomes a national park

1922   Mary Colter's Phantom Ranch opens

1933   Civilian Conservation Corps is created and does major construction projects at Grand Canyon and other national parks

World Timeline

2 billion years ago.   The first cells develop into complex cells or eukaryotes.

220-65 million years ago.   Age of Dinosaurs

65 million years ago.   Extinction of the dinosaurs which leads to the evolution of primates and organisms living in trees.

13-7 million years ago.   Hominins evolve, paving the way for the first humans to come soon after.

1500   Portuguese navigator Pedro Alvarez Cabral discovers South America and lands in present day Brazil.

1536   King Henry VIII executes second wife, Anne Boleyn.

1869   First United States transcontinental rail route is completed.

1893   New Zealand becomes the first country to give women the right to vote.

1900   Congress passes the Lacey Act, which provides criminal penalties for those illegally taking game, fish or plant life and attempt to profit from it.

1903   The Wright brothers fly the first powered, controlled, heavier-than-air plane at Kitty Hawk, North Carolina.

1908   Ford Motor Company produces the Model T.

1914   World War I begins.

1916   National Park Service is founded.

1922   BBC (British Broadcasting Corporation) begins radio service from the Macaroni House in the United Kingdom

Grand Canyon Timeline (cont.)

1933 Mary Colter's Desert View Watchtower opens

1937 Buzz Holmstrom does first solo boat trip through Grand Canyon

1938 Norm Nevills begins commercial river running in Grand Canyon

1952 Georgie White begins using rubber rafts for Grand Canyon trips

1956 For first time, one million people visit Grand Canyon National Park

1966 U. S. Bureau of Reclamation proposes building dams inside Grand Canyon. Sierra Club leads and wins fight against dams.

1974 Grand Canyon National Park begins shuttle bus system

1975 President Gerald Ford signs bill nearly doubling size of Grand Canyon National Park

2000 New park Visitor Center opens

2016 100th anniversary of National Park Service. More than five million people visit Grand Canyon National Park

World Timeline (cont.)

1933   Wiley Post succeeds in finishing the first round-the-world solo flight.

1937   The Golden Gate Bridge in San Francisco, California opens to pedestrian traffic, and is the longest spanning bridge to date.

1937   King George VI is coronated after his brother, Duke Edward of Windsor, steps down from the throne.

1939   World War II begins.

1952   The Big Bang Theory is proposed in Physical Review.

1956   The U.S.'s own actress, Grace Kelly, marries the Prince Rainier III of Monaco.

1966   The Catholic and Anglican churches meet officially for the first time in 400 years.

1970   First Earth Day. National Park Service begins managing national parks with more emphasis on protecting ecosystems.

1979   Margaret Thatcher becomes the first female British Prime Minister and, to this day, the longest ruling prime minister in the country's history.

2001   World Trade Centers in New York are attacked by terrorists.

2016   Businessman Donald Trump elected 45th president of the United States, highlighting deep political divisions within country.

Glossary

Abstract   Difficult to understand

Acrobatic   Being good at jumping, balancing, tumbling, and swinging from or on things

Adapted   Changed to fit a new use or situation

Burro   A donkey

Cacti   Plural of cactus, a plant specially adapted to survive in dry areas. Cacti have fleshy stems and branches with prickles or needles.

Chaotic   Complete confusion

Cleats   A device attached to shoes to prevent slipping

Conquistador   A leader in the Spanish conquest of the Americas

Conservationist   A person who wants to protect nature, wild plants, and wild animals

Dehydrate   To lose bodily fluids

Drought   A long period of dry weather

Erode   Gradually worn away, usually by water

Fault   A break in the Earth's crust

Flash floods   A flood, caused by heavy rainfall, that happens quickly

Fossil   The remains of a plant or animal that has been buried and turned into rock

Geology   The science that studies rocks and the history of Earth

Geyser   A spring that sometimes erupts water

Hogan   A traditional Navajo house, with eight sides

Locomotive   A train engine for pulling other train cars

Mules   A mix between a donkey and a horse

National Park Service   A government agency dedicated to protecting and staffing National Parks and National Monuments

Nebula   A huge cloud of gas or dust in space

Pictograph   A drawing on a rock wall from native people

Primitive   Lacking advanced technology and knowledge

Prospector   A person who explores an area in search of valuable resources like gold or oil

Prosthetic   An artifical replacement for a missing body part like a leg or arm

Reservation   An area of public lands saved for a specific purpose, as for use by Native Americans

Schist   A type of rock with crystal patterns

Stirrups   A pair of metal rings hung from a saddle to support the feet of a horseback rider

Strip Mine   A mine created by stripping away or removing unwanted materials

Tall Tale   An exaggerated story

Tarantula   A large hairy spider

Tectonic plate   Earth's crust is divided into several large sections, which move around

Trilobites   An extinct animal from the prehistoric ocean

Bibliography

Berke, Arnold. *Mary Colter: Architect of the Southwest*. New York: Princeton Architectural Press, 2002.

Farabee, Charles R. Jr. *National Park Ranger: An American Icon*. Lanham, MD: Roberts Reinhart Publishers, 2003.

Lago, Don. *Grand Canyon: A History of a Natural Wonder and National Park*. Reno, NV: University of Nevada Press, 2015.

Leavengood, Betty. *Grand Canyon Women: Lives Shapes by Landscape*. Grand Canyon, AZ: Grand Canyon Association, 2004.

Naylor, Roger. *The Amazing Kolb Brothers of Grand Canyon*. Grand Canyon, AZ: Grand Canyon Association, 2017.

Powell, John Wesley. *The Exploration of the Colorado River and its Canyons*. New York: Penguin Books, 1987.

Ranney, Wayne. *Carving Grand Canyon: Evidence, Theories, and Mystery*. Grand Canyon, AZ: Grand Canyon Association, 2012.

Further Reading

Graf, Mike. *Tail of the Scorpion*. Golden, CO: Fulcrum Publishing, 2006.

Lamb, Susan. *Grand Canyon Wildlife: Rim to River*. Grand Canyon, AZ: Grand Canyon Association, 2013.

Henry, Marguerite. *Brighty of the Grand Canyon*. Chicago: Rand McNally, 1953.

Robson, Gary D., and Elijah Brady Clark. *Who Pooped in the Park? Grand Canyon National Park: Scat and Tracks for Kids*. Helena, MT: Farcountry Press, 2005.

Ross, Michael Elsohn. *Exploring the Earth with John Wesley Powell*. Minneapolis, MN: Carolrhonda Books, 2000.

Index